CAPTURED AMERICAN & BRITISH TANKS

A Sherman VC Firefly

UNDER THE GERMAN FLAG

WERNER REGENBERG

GW00537175

Schiffer Military/Aviation History
Atglen, PA

The First Captured Tanks

The idea of putting captured tanks into service to increase one's own fighting strength was already utilized by the Germans in World War I. In March of 1918 the Captured Tank Unit 11, equipped with British Mark IV tanks, went into service as the first captured-tank unit in military history. Until the end of World War I, six tank units (11 to 16) were set up, using captured British Mark IV tanks, each unit having only five of the captured tanks.

Left: The 1./Panzer Regiment 5 seems to have captured a Sherman tank in Tunis. It was sent to the Army Weapons Office.

Translated from the German by Edward Force.

This book originally appeared under the title, *Beutepanzer unterm Balkenkreuz - Amerikanische und englische Kampfpanzer*, by Podzun-Pallas Verlag, Friedberg.

Printed in the United States of America.
ISBN: 0-88740-524-X

We are interested in hearing from authors with book ideas on related topics.

Published by Schiffer Publishing Ltd.
77 Lower Valley Road
Atglen, PA 19310
Please write for a free catalog.
This book may be purchased from the publisher.
Please include $2.95 postage.
Try your bookstore first.

Photo Credits

German Federal Archives (BA)
RAC Tank Museum (RAC)
Jörn Dzingel (JD)
Richard Eiermann (RE)
Wolfgang Fleischer (WF)
Title Page: Horst Helmus
Thomas L. Jentz (TLJ)
Klaus Jordan (KJ)
H. Lohse (HL)
Karl Heinz Münch (KHM)
Regis Potie (RP)
Franz-Josef Schäfer (FJS)
Horst Scheibert (HS)
Wolfgang Schneider (WSN)
Walter Spielberger (WSP)
Bernd Wittgayer (BW)

With the beginning of the western campaign on May 10, 1940, German and British tanks faced each other for the first time since 1918. On this important day the order of battle for the British Expeditionary Corps showed the following strength in battle tanks:

342 Mark VI Light Tanks, 150 Cruiser Tanks, and 77 Matilda I Infantry Tanks. By June 4, most of these tanks were destroyed or had fallen undamaged into German hands. The British cited their total losses in France as follows:

407 Mark VI Light Tanks, 158 Cruiser Tanks, and 126 Infantry Tanks.

Only six Mark VI Light Tanks and seven Cruiser Tanks could be taken back to Britain.

But how many of these 691 British tanks lost in the western campaign could be put into service by German troops?

To this day no definite statistics have become known, thus we must rely on estimations.

More than half the numbers of almost all types of French tanks used in the western campaign were captured in usable condition, and it can be assumed from this fact that the situation with British tanks must have been similar. That means that some 200 light Mark VI, 80 Cruisers and 65 Infantry Tanks could have been used by the German Wehrmacht.

Some of the captured tanks were sent to the Army Weapons Office for examination and shooting tests. There it was determined what fighting value these vehicles had and with which weapons they could be attacked. Firing tables for tank guns and antitank guns were made up after firing tests, showing where the enemy tanks could be struck most easily.

Since the supply of ammunition and spare parts for the captured British tanks was not as dependable as for the French tanks, whose ammunition and production factories were also captured, a goodly number of the British tanks had to be scrapped to keep others in service. For example, ammunition was available only in very limited quantities.

Since the tanks' readiness for action could, for the reasons stated above, never be assured, most captured British tanks were turned over to training units. There these vehicles were used for tank-fighting practice until they were worn out and found their last use as targets on the firing ranges.

Another possible use for these vehicles was as full-track towing tractors or as chassis for self-propelled guns or other support vehicles.

Because of the lack of ammunition and spare parts, only a few British tanks captured in the western campaign were used by German units without being modified.

At the beginning of 1941, the Captured Tank Company (e) was established, using captured British tanks. The company consisted of at least one light platoon (probably Mark VI), two platoons with Cruiser Tanks, one workshop group and one supply column. On February 11, 1941, though, the order was given to dissolve this Captured Tank Company. What remained of it became part of Panzer Unit (F) 100, which still reported nine Cruiser Tanks (A 13) as ready for action on June 1, 1941. To judge by the available photographs, the Cruiser Tanks of this unit still took part in the attack on the Soviet Union.

After the western campaign, the captured tanks left on the battlefield first had to be collected and inspected. This was done by captured tank staffs at the so-called captured tank assembly bases. This picture shows an abandoned Vickers Mark VIB. (WSP)

Captured tanks were dismantled and given a general overhaul in French workshops. In the process, a goodly number of these vehicles were scrapped to provide spare parts for other tanks. At the same time, workshop personnel were trained to use captured tanks.

In mid-1941 Artillery Regiment 227 gained a 15th Assault Battery of self-propelled guns. Mark VI tanks were rebuilt with 10.5 cm light field howitzers for this battery, while others were made into armored reconnaissance cars.

The Kummersdorf Test Center of the Army Weapons Office reported, on April 1, 1941, their numbers of British tanks as three Mark VI-C, nine Cruiser Tanks and three Infantry Tanks.

In mid-1942 twelve more Mark VI tanks were rebuilt as armored ammunition carriers for a new armored artillery brigade.

In addition, as early as mid-1940, various infantry divisions and other army units in France gave instruction in the use of British tracked and armored vehicles, including training on the Mark VI. This was probably done in view of the planned invasion of the British Isles, so that captured equipment could be used immediately by the invading troops.

It is not known how many British tanks were captured during the Balkan campaign of 1941. Captured Matilda Mark II infantry tanks were used in Crete for several years by Panzer Unit 212 (Crete).

Additional British tanks fell into German hands during the African campaign. The Panzer-Armee Afrika constantly suffered from supply shortages and made use of everything it captured, from tobacco and canned fruit to tanks and other motor vehicles. At times, the Panzer-Armee Afrika's complement of motor vehicles was composed of up to 85% captured vehicles.

Platoons of captured tanks were set up in Panzer Regiment 8 and later in Panzer Engineer Battalion 33 of the 15th Panzer Division, in Panzer Regiment 5 of the 21st Panzer Division, and Panzerjäger Unit 605 of the 90th Light African Division.

In addition, individual captured tanks saw service with other units in Africa.

On February 12, 1942, the Panzer-Armee Afrika ordered the establishment of a captured tank unit using British and American tanks. The unit was given the name "Pz.Abt. zbV Panzer-Armee Afrika." Probably the captured equipment was not sufficient to set up a whole unit, for on March 28, 1942 it was ordered that the captured tanks of the Abt. zbV were to belong to the combat echelon of the Pz.AOK Afrika as of April 1, 1942. There the captured tanks saw service, until the surrender of the Pz.AOK in Tunis, as the 2./Kampfstaffel of the Commander of the Panzer-Armee Afrika. The company was equipped with up to eighteen captured tanks, and after several vehicles were lost, it was constantly refilled with new captured equipment. In general, these were Mark III "Valentine" (about twelve) and Mark VI "Crusader" (about four), and the company also had up to five armored reconnaissance cars. The Mark III tanks were captured early in 1942 without bolts, aiming scopes and radios. These lacking parts were sent from Germany at the end of May and installed early in June. This was possible because Cruiser and Matilda II tanks captured in the western campaign used the same two-pound tank gun as the Mark III "Valentines" and Mark VI "Crusaders" captured in Africa.

The tanks of the 2./Kampfstaffel Pz.AOK Afrika were used for infantry support, reconnaissance, securing and as vehicles for artillery observers. The company's Mark III and Mark VI tanks also fought battles with British Mark III and Mark VI tanks, in which both sides shot down the other's tanks. In a low-level air attack on October 24, 1942, seven of the company's twelve captured tanks were total losses, and the other five had to undergo repairs.

Of the light M3A3 Stuart tanks delivered by the USA as of mid-1941, the M3 "Lee" and "Grant" tanks that first appeared in 1942, and the Sherman tanks that arrived at the end of 1942, only a few examples fell into German hands. The situation was exactly the same for the American tanks after they landed in North Africa in November of 1942. In May of 1943 the war ended in Africa.

Since many new British and American tanks saw service in Africa, everything possible was done to capture at least one example of each and send it back to the Army Weapons Office and its Weapon Testing Office in Germany for testing. The story of an American Sherman tank known as "War Daddy II" is well known. It was captured near Sbeitla, Tunisia by the 1st Company of Panzer Unit 501 on February 22, 1943. The tank was then taken to Tunis in a land march that covered more than 350 kilometers in four and a half days, and loaded onto a ship there. As many photos attest, it reached the Army Weapons Office in good condition and ready for action.

Another possibility of obtaining British and American tanks occurred in the Russian theater of war. Since the beginning of 1942, Lend-Lease tanks had arrived there. Other than individual tanks used by various units, the existence of only one captured tank platoon is known; it used five Russian Sherman tanks.

In the attempted landing on the coast near Dieppe on August 19, 1942, 23 Churchill tanks were captured. Some of the vehicles were made operational and turned over to the Army Weapons Office for testing. Two of the Churchills remained with captured tank units for a long time, in fact until the beginning of 1944, when shortages of spare parts and ammunition resulted in their being used as targets for firing drills.

The Allied landing in Normandy took place on June 6, 1944, and despite being driven back steadily, the German forces were able to capture individual British and American tanks. The American Sherman tanks were particularly prized, and some were used by the Wehrmacht in captured tank platoons. Probably the best-known use of captured Shermans was that by Panzer Brigade 150. This unit, established in November 1944, was to push forward beyond the Allied front in the Ardennes offensive and cause confusion there. For this purpose, the brigade was equipped as much as possible with captured equipment. Shortages of captured equipment were made up with "disguised" German equipment. For example, Panther tanks were "disguised" as American M-36 tank destroyers with sheet-metal panels. Panzer Brigade 150 is said to have possessed ten Sherman tanks.

As early as October 1940, the Army Office had issued a command stating that two examples of every captured tank, motor vehicle, etc., were to be

A Sherman M4 tank of the French First Army is being towed away by a Panther recovery vehicle. The M4A2, known as "Malakoff", was captured by the Heavy Panzerjäger Unit 654 in the vicinity of Heiteren, Alsace, late in 1944. At the end of 1944 and early in 1945 the Heavy Panzerjäger Unit 654 used a Sherman tank as a full-tracked towing tractor. (KHM)

turned over for evaluation purposes. The captured tanks were sent to the Motor Vehicle Test Center of the Army Weapons Office's Test Section in Kummersdorf. Tanks tested there were sent on to the Tank Museum of the Army Vehicle Office in Stettin-Altdamm. An order of the High Command of the Army Group Vistula on March 9, 1945 authorized the removal of the captured tanks from this museum for use in the defense of Stettin.

It is probable that several captured American and British tanks also saw service there.

Before and during the war, the Army Weapons Office collected information on the weapons of other countries and published so-called "Kennblätter Fremdgerät" (information sheets on foreign equipment) to help identify the weapons. Here a system was used that first stated the German name of the equipment, followed by an identification number and a letter in parentheses indicating the country of origin. Numbers in the 700's were used for tanks, and thus the designation of, for example, the American Sherman medium tank was: Panzerkampfwagen M4 748 (a) and that of the British Mark II "Matilda" infantry tank was: Infanterie Panzerkampfwagen Mk II 748 (e).

The identification numbers were given as soon as any information on a tank, such as a newspaper article, was available. A captured specimen did not have to be at hand.

The troops did not usually use these designations in their entirety, usually calling the captured tanks just "Matilda" or "Mark II." A vehicle with the designation of Mark II was thus not always identified clearly. It could, for example, be a Cruiser Mark II tank, a Matilda Mark II, or a Valentine Mark II.

In this book the tanks will be presented in the order of their German identification numbers.

Left: in March of 1944, these two M4 tanks were captured near Nettuno, Italy. They were the 12th and 15th vehicles of C Company of the 756th Armored Regiment of the American 5th Armored Division. The tanks had just been captured and had not yet been given German markings. (BA)

Right: The Matilda II infantry tank as a display and test vehicle of the Army Weapons Office. This tank, with the British number T.6910 now bears the Wehrmacht number plate WH-0170638. (BA)

American Tanks

During the war years of 1939 to 1945, the USA built a total of 88,410 tanks. Large numbers of them were turned over to allied countries, including Great Britain, the Soviet Union, France and Canada. Only a few American tanks were captured by German forces.

LIGHT TANK M3(a) "STUART"

The M3 was developed out of the M2A4, the standard American light tank at the beginning of World War II, in July of 1940. Its armament consisted of a 3.7 cm tank gun in the turret with coaxial 7.62 mm machine guns, two 7.62 mm machine guns in casemates to the right and left, one 7.62 mm bow machine gun, and one 7.62 mm anti-aircraft machine gun in the turret. The taw casemate machine guns were often not installed. With a main armor of 44.5 mm, the tank weighed 13 tons.

The crew consisted of four men, and the speed was 58 kph. The American Car and Foundry Company produced a large series of 5811 M3 tanks by August 1942. The M3A1 successor model had an improved welded turret without a commander's cupola. 4621 tanks of this version were produced. The M3A3 was created by means of large-scale redesigning of the hull, casemates and turret, and 3427 of them were built. With that the M3 series attained a total production of 13,859 tanks by October 9143.

The Americans turned a large number of M3 tanks over to the British, who used them in North Africa as of June 1941. Because of its technical reliability, the M3 was nicknamed "Honey" by the British. The 3.7 cm tank gun had sufficient firepower to take on the German Panzer III and IV tanks. Thanks to its high speed, the "Stuart" version was also very mobile.

When the American troops landed in Tunisia, additional M3 and successor tanks arrived in Africa.

As photographs show, captured M3 tanks were put into service by the German troops, though only in small numbers.

The Soviet Union obtained 1676 "Stuart" tanks and used them against the Wehrmacht. Several were captured and generally used as tracked towing tractors, as by StuG. Abt. 197. The further development of the M3 led directly to the M5 light tank. This light tank was used against the Wehrmacht by the Americans in Africa as well as in Europe after the invasion. Scarcely any M5 light tanks fell into German hands.

A light M3 (a) tank, used by the British forces in North Africa as of July 1942 and nicknamed "Honey." This tank has an older-type angular turret. The openings for the casemate machine guns are covered by angular armor plates. The only German marking is the cross on the side.

Left: another ex-British M3 "Honey" in German service. The turret has the later rounded shape, and the casemate machine-gun openings are covered by round armor plates. The German cross is painted with wider arms. This vehicle, like the other "Honey", also seems to have been abandoned by its new owners. (WSN)

Right: Even though not much can be recognized, this photo shows (at far right) an ex-Russian M3, which belonged to Assault Gun Unit 197 along with a Stalinez full-track towing tractor. The Assault Gun Unit 197 utilized captured M3 tanks to tow their assault guns. (KHM)

Left: The successor of the M3 light tank was the M5. The M5 shown here was captured by the Germans after the Allied landing in Normandy and has changed hands a second time. The captured tank, now marked with German crosses, is fitted with a "Cullin Hedgerow Device" on the bow, with which the tanks could cut their way through the hedges of Normandy.

It soon became clear to the Americans that their light tanks with 3.7 cm guns were too weak for modern warfare. A tank with a 7.5 cm gun was called for, and the Procurement Office gave it the designation of M3. The M3 was ordered from the drawing board and produced in series as of August 1941. The armament of the M3 "Lee" consisted of a 75mm tank gun in a casemate, a 3.7 cm gun with a coaxial 7.62 mm machine gun in the turret, a 7.62 mm machine gun in a cupola on top of the turret, and two 7.62 mm machine guns in the bow. The tank had a seven-man crew and attained a speed of 42 kph. The armor was 37 mm thick; the weight was 29 tons.

By December 1942, 6258 M3 tanks in various forms (M3A1, M3A2, M3A3, M3A4 and M3A5) had been built.

The British ordered M3 tanks with a turret of their own design from the Americans. This turret had more room inside, enough to house a radio set, and no cupola or machine gun. The crew of this M3, called the "Grant", was only six men. 2887 M3 tanks of the "Lee" and "Grant" types were delivered to Great Britain. They first saw service at the battle of Gazala, in Africa, on March 27, 1942. All earlier British tanks could fire only armor-piercing ammunition. With the Grant and its 7.5 cm howitzer, a vehicle was available for the first time that could fire both armor-piercing and explosive shells.

The Soviet Union received 1386 M3A3 tanks through the Lend-Lease program. Some of them were captured by the Wehrmacht, but no units equipped with M3 tanks appear to have been set up.

Left: This M3 "General Grant" was captured from the British 8th Army in North Africa and then shipped to Kummersdorf. On its side, the M3 bears the lettering "O.K.H. Kummersdorf Krafs Stelle." The armor-plate thicknesses and angles of this vehicle were measured. The General Grant had a British-designed turret. (BA)

Right: There were 1386 M3 tanks delivered to the soviet Union. This tank was later used by a German unit. The photo, taken near Mzensk in February of 1943, shows an M3 tank in white winter camouflage. The small white German cross on the left side can scarcely be seen. (RE)

Above and below: Another M3 captured in Russia in 1942 is this vehicle with the American number U.S.A. W-304,850. The tank with turret number 147 has had German crosses carefully painted on it, which suggests that it was used by the fighting forces. Written on the side in chalk is "Do not scrap." This inscription was very important, since the troops could use any and all spare parts and were happy to dismantle captured vehicles for their parts. The vehicle makes a splendid impression and appears to be fully functional. (BA)

Above: two M3 tanks at a collecting base in Russia, during the summer of 1942. The two tanks are marked "Confiscated O.K.H. /Ag.K. II, to be loaded with other tanks and sent to the Army Subsidiary Goods Depot in Stettin." The tank at the left is equipped with a counterweight to stabilize the 7.5 cm tank gun. (BA)

Below: This M3 tank marked W-304,850 found its way from the eastern front to the Army Weapons Office, where it was marked with information as to its armor strength and the angles of the armor plates. Behind the German cross on the right side, the lettering "do not scrap" can still be seen. (BA)

PANZERKAMPFWAGEN M4 748 (a)
"SHERMAN"

One day after the decision to produce the M3 medium tank, the developmental work on a new medium tank began. This was the M4, better known as the "Sherman" tank.

The M4 had a 7.5 cm tank gun and a coaxial 7.62 mm machine gun in a turret that could turn 360 degrees. Another 7.62 mm machine gun was installed in the bow. Some of the tanks were also equipped with a 12.7 mm anti-aircraft machine gun on top of the turret. The hull armor was 51 mm thick, the turret armor 76 mm. Additional armor plate sometimes reinforced the normal armor to 100 mm. These vehicles, weighing 32 tons, reached a speed of 42 kph and had a five-man crew.

More M4 Sherman tanks were built than any other American tank. In all, 49,230 Shermans of a wide variety of types were produced.

The M4 version (6748 built) had a welded superstructure, the M4A1 model (6281 built), on the other hand, had a cast upper body.

The M4A3 version also had a welded upper body and was essentially identical to. There were major differences in the engine cover and the rear of the hull. The M4A3 was the most frequently built type in the series.

Only the major differences between individual versions have been noted here. Constant improvements to individual versions resulted in thousands of actual variants.

The M4M3E2 was an assault tank with particularly heavy bow armor (101 mm) and an especially heavily armored cast turret (178 mm). It was armed with the standard 7.5 cm tank gun.

To increase the tank's fighting value, and particularly its firepower, several Sherman tanks of the M4A1 and M4A3 series were equipped with a different turret (T23) and a 7.6 cm tank gun. To improve the tank's driving characteristics, a different type of running gear with coil springs and wider tracks was installed toward the end of the war. To indicate the difference, these vehicles were given the suffix "HVSS." On account of their developmental number M4A3E8, they were also nicknamed "Easy Eight." They were all armed with the 7.6 cm tank gun.

4680 vehicles of the M4 and M4A3 types were equipped with a 10.5 cm howitzer for fire support.

The British Army received 17,181 Sherman tanks from the Americans. Some of the Shermans were equipped with the British 17-pound gun and designated "M4 Sherman VC Firefly."

The German Wehrmacht encountered their first Shermans in Africa in October of 1942. These were vehicles delivered to the British under Lend-Lease terms. After the Allies landed in Algeria, the first American units with Sherman tanks also came into contact with the German troops.

In the Lend-Lease agreement, 4252 Sherman tanks were also delivered to the Soviet Union. They were the M4A2 version, with welded hulls and Diesel engines, which were only turned over to allies. These tanks were equipped roughly half and half with 7.5 cm and 7.6 cm tank guns. Some Shermans with 7.5 cm guns were fitted with the 7.62 cm gun of the T34 tank by the Russians.

Tank no. 15 of C Company, 756th Armored Regiment, US Army, captured near Nettuno, Italy, in 1944. It is an early version of an M4 with a three-piece screwed-on gearbox cover at the bow. (BA)

The French armed forces were also supplied to some extent with Sherman tanks.

The Wehrmacht captured its first Shermans in Tunisia and shipped them back to Germany for the Army Weapons Office to examine.

The greatest numbers of Sherman tanks, though, fell into German hands in France after the 1944 invasion. Many units were able to set up a captured tank unit and equip it with Shermans. The use of this tank is documented for the 21st Panzer Division (four tanks), 25th Panzer Grenadier Division (four), the 10th SS Panzer Division "Frundsberg" (ten), Panzer Brigade 150 (ten), and the 5th Parachute Jäger Division (six). There were individual tanks in many other units.

In August of 1944, the Captured Tank Company 281 established a platoon of five Sherman tanks (with 7.5 cm guns) that had been captured in Russia.

Among the German troops, the Sherman tank with the 7.5 cm gun was known as the "Sherman short" and the type with the 7.6 cm gun as the "Sherman long."

On March 31, 1945, the Panzer Company "Berka" was set up, using the tanks of the Berka Test Center. It had three Jagdpanzer 38 tanks (one of them with a recoilless gun), one Panzer IV, two Panzer III, two Sherman short and one Sherman long. When the unit was established, each of the Sherman tanks carried 50 rounds of ammunition.

At the same time, the Panzer Company "Kummersdorf" was established at the Kummersdorf Test Center, using an even greater assortment of tanks. In this company, two Sherman long tanks were used by a conditionally mobile platoon.

These were probably the last units established with captured tanks.

Above: Tank no. 12 with a German commander. The picture clearly shows the stern of the M4 with its double doors ahead of the engine compartment. (BA)

Below: American soldiers in their M10 Tank Destroyer have come upon a Sherman tank with German markings. The crosses were painted very hastily without a stencil. The tank is a Sherman M4A3 with a long 7.6 cm gun. (BA)

Left: This Sherman M4A1 was captured by the First Company, Panzer Unit 501, near Sbeitla, Tunisia, on February 22, 1943. The tank, nicknamed "War Daddy II", belonged to G Company of the 3rd Battalion of the 1st American Armored Division. The Sherman was shipped from Tunisia to Germany for the Army Weapons Office, where this picture was taken. The tanks in the Weapons Office's display collection were given number plates for exhibitions; otherwise this was not customary for army tanks. This Sherman bears the number WH-058 941. (BA)

Right: In the spring of 1944, this M4A1 was captured in Italy. It is likewise an early version with a three-piece screwed-on bow. The tank belonged to the 751st US Armored Regiment and was then put to use by the 3rd Panzer Grenadier Division. (BA)

Left: The Sherman was used by the unit to train tank-destroyer forces in antitank warfare. In the foreground is a raised position for infantry, made according to the textbook. (BA)

Left: A snowed-in Sherman M4A3 in the Ardennes in January of 1945. The tank is carefully marked with German crosses, making it easy to recognize as being captured. It was captured by the 5th Paratroop Jäger Division, which had six captured Sherman tanks.

Right: Two British soldiers examine captured-back Sherman tanks that have been fitted with additional armor plate on their bow, sides and turret and marked with a goodly number of German crosses. In the center is a Sherman VC Firefly with a British 7.6 cm tank gun; behind it is an M4 with a 7.5 cm gun, and in front is an M4A3. (WSN)

Left: The wreck of another M4A3 with a long 7.6 cm gun, briefly in German service. The American star is still on the turret, but a German cross has been painted on the side. This Sherman had a 7.6 cm tank gun and a different turret (T 23) than the vehicles with the standard armament. (WSN)

Above and below: Soldiers of the 1st SS Panzer Corps "Leibstandarte" with a Sherman Firefly captured from the 7th British Tank Division in Normandy in 1944. The tank, numbered T 212728, belonged to an A company, as the triangle on the turret indicates. The tank took a hit on the turret shield and is being examined for usability or usable parts. (BA)

Above and below: This captured Sherman VC Firefly, with serial number T 148532, was examined to see what types of steel were used to make it. The letter G stands for cast and W for rolled steel. The only German marking is a white cross painted on the sides of the turret. The triangle to the right of the cross is a British symbol for an A company. (BA)

Above: A photo of the Sherman VC Firefly that was used as a model for the cover picture of this volume. It was produced in America, armed with British weapons, and captured from British or American forces. (BA)

Below: The same tank, seen from the other side. The newly applied camouflage paint can be seen clearly. (BA)

Above: The same tank running cross-country at top speed. German crosses have been painted carefully on the turret and sides. The box on the rear of the turret is typical of British Sherman tanks. (BA)

Below: The same Sherman Firefly again. A general and another officer are examining the armor. The ball-shaped muzzle brake on the British 7.6 cm tank gun is easy to see. (BA)

Both pages:

The German crew of a Sherman Firefly, an Oberleutnant, a Feldwebel, an Unteroffizier and a Gefreite, get accustomed to the new vehicle. It is the same tank shown on the previous page.

Of particular interest are the (five!) German crosses around the turret, which show how carefully captured tanks were marked. The number and size of the German crosses are typical of captured tanks. (BA)

CAPTURED BRITISH TANKS

Since World War I there has been a traditional differentiation in Britain between infantry-support tanks and battle tanks for operative warfare. Tanks made for actual tank battles against enemy tanks have also been referred to as cavalry tanks. There have also been light armored vehicles for armed reconnaissance.

MARK VI LIGHT TANK

These light battle tanks, made by the firm of Vickers, were developed from the Carden-Loyd series in 1929. The Mark I to Mark VIA types saw service only in the British Isles. The expeditionary corps in France used the Mark VIB (about 350) and Mark VIC (about 60) types. In all, about 1000 light tanks of the Mark I to Mark VIC types were built. In addition to France, they were also captured in Greece, Crete and North Africa.

The Mark VIB Light Tank built as of 1936 was designated "leichter Panzerkampfwagen Mk VIB 735 (e)" by the Germans. This tank, with a three-man crew, was armed with a 12.7 mm machine gun and a coaxial 7.7 mm Vickers machine gun in the turret. The 5.2-ton vehicle attained a speed of 48 kph; its armor was 14 mm thick.

The successor model, the Mk VIC Light Tank, had air-cooled BESA machine guns in place of the Vickers type. This tank, designated "leichter Panzerkampfwagen Mk VIC 736 (e)" by the Germans, was armed with one 15 mm and one coaxial 7.92 mm machine gun. The vehicle can be distinguished from the Mk VIB easily by its long 15 mm machine gun and its lack of a commander's cupola.

The Mark VI tanks captured in France were utilized without modification in schools and training centers for testing purposes and teaching aids in antitank training.

Seven Mark VI tanks were rebuilt into "10.5-cm-le-FH-16 auf Geschützwagen Mk VI (e)" howitzers, and four other Mark VI into "Beobachtungspanzer auf Fahrgestell Mk VI (e)" armored reconnaissance cars. Both types saw service in Russia with the 15th Assault Battery of Artillery Regiment 227.

Another twelve Mark VI tanks were rebuilt into armored "Munitionspanzer auf Fahrgestell Mk VI (e)" ammunition carriers and saw service with the armored artillery brigade in France.

This Vickers Mark VI tank captured in the western campaign was turned over to the police for antitank training. The Police Weapons School III in The Hague equipped the Type VIB tank with a 7.92 cm MG 08 in its turret. Many obsolete tanks were utilized by training units.

Left: A captured Vickers Mark VIB light tank in North Africa in 1941. The vehicle bears the typical blue and brown stripe camouflage used on British armored vehicles at that time. A German cross has been painted on the turret above the triangle of the A company. A swastika flag affords further identification. (BW)

Right: This Vickers Mark VIC light tank with number T 5975 (T stands for tank) was turned over to the Army Weapons Office and added to its collection of display and test vehicles. The vehicle bore the Wehrmacht registration number WH-0135041. The Vickers VIC is easily told from the VIB type by the long BESA machine gun. (WSP)

Left: The installation of 10.5 cm leFH 16 howitzers on Vickers Mark VI chassis was carried out by A.R. 227 in mid-1941. The attempts were satisfactory and led to the establishment of an assault battery with six 10.5 cm leFH 16 guns on Mark VI (e) chassis. Here is an early test vehicle seen during test firing of the light howitzer. (WSP)

Left: By rearmoring the fighting compartment, a self-propelled gun car was created whose looks and layout pointed the way to future self-propelled guns used by the Wehrmacht. To react to the gun's recoil better, the guns were fitted with ground jacks at the rear. (WSP)

Right: In this version of the 10.5 cm leFH 16 on Mark VI (e) chassis, the armor protection of the gun and the fighting compartment has been improved even more. The exhaust system has also been rebuilt. The vehicle bears the markings of the assault battery of A.R. 227 of the 227th Infantry Division. (WSP)

Left: A look into the gun compartment of this vehicle. At the left front is the gunner's seat, with targeting optics and aiming gear, behind it the commander's seat with shear periscope. At right are two seats for loaders, who also use the MG 34 machine gun. With the driver, the crew numbered five men.

Above: Also in the assault battery of A.R. 227 were four observation tanks on Mark VI (3) chassis. These observation vehicles were made by removing the turret and mounting the commander's cupola of the Mark VIB directly on the upper part of the body. These vehicles were not armed.

Below: Another rebuilt vehicle using the chassis of the Vickers Mark VI light tank was an ammunition carrier. Here the turret was removed and a boxlike superstructure added. Every carrier had an ammunition trailer. This is an ammunition carrier of the armored A.R. 1 (Sfl.). (2 x WSP)

MK I 747 (e) "MATILDA I" INFANTRY TANK

The first tank that was developed purely for infantry support was the Infantry Tank Mark I "Matilda I" of the Vickers firm. This vehicle, equipped with only one Vickers 12.7 mm machine gun, had 60 mm armor and a top speed of only 12 kph. A higher speed was not required, since the infantry was supposed to follow the vehicle. The crew consisted of two men.

In all, 139 "Matilda I" tanks were built, 97 of which saw service with the Expeditionary Corps in France. All 97 vehicles were lost and were either destroyed or fell into German hands ready for action.

Two vehicles in good working order were on hand at the Kummersdorf test center of the Army Weapons Office for examination and testing purposes at the beginning of 1941. No other use of this underpowered and underarmed tank by German forces is known.

This Matilda I infantry tank was acquired by the Army Weapons Office. Ninety-seven of these vehicles, armed only with a 12.7 mm machine gun, saw service with the British Expeditionary Corps in France and Belgium.

MK II 748 (e) "MATILDA II" INFANTRY TANK

As soon as the first prototypes of the "Matilda I" were built, efforts were made to upgrade its armor and armament. From these considerations there arose the "Matilda II", made by the Vulcan Foundry. The vehicle, powered by two Diesel engines, weighed 24 tons and reached a maximum speed of 24 kph. It was armed with a 4 cm tank gun and coaxial machine gun. The crew numbered four men, and the armor measured 70 mm.

The British Expeditionary Corps lost 29 "Matilda II" tanks in France.

Again, two of these vehicles were utilized for testing purposes by the Army Weapons Office.

Another "Matilda II", with turret number 111, was used for loading practice by the High Seas Instructional Command at Terneuzen. At the end of 1942, the vehicle's turret was removed and a 5 cm KwK L/42 gun was installed on a pivot mount. This vehicle, nicknamed "Oswald", was also armed with two 08/15 machine guns.

All six "Matilda II" tanks that the British had on Crete were captured during the invasion of Crete in 1941 and taken over by the Panzer Unit 212, which was organized there. In mid-1943 the vehicles were still reported among the unit's equipment.

The "Matilda II" saw considerable service with the German units in Africa.

The 15th Panzer Division included a captured tank platoon, with up to seven "Matilda II" tanks in service, as part of Panzer Regiment 8 from June to August of 1941. At the end of August 1941, these tanks were turned over to Panzer Engineer Battalion 33, and the active strength of the platoon until the end of November 1941 included two to five "Matilda II" tanks.

In the 21st Panzer Division too, there was a captured tank platoon, with five "Matilda II" tanks, in Panzer Regiment 5 in June of 1941. From July to August, though, only one such vehicle was at hand.

A few "Matilda II" tanks were also captured in Russia. The Russians had obtained 1084 "Matilda II" tanks through the Lend-Lease program.

All three photos show the same captured Matilda II tank in North Africa. The tank, painted the color of sand, is marked with German crosses on its turret and also carries a swastika flag. Since the crosses are painted only on the turret, it might be difficult to recognize it as a German tank. Thus a ground panel with a swastika has been tied onto the front of the turret.

This tank was probably captured and used by Panzer Regiment 8. (1 x BA, 1 x WS)

Left: A captured Matilda II beside a Ford truck of the 21st Panzer Division in North Africa. It may have been captured by Panzer Regiment 5. The tank is marked very clearly with German crosses.

Right: The same tank, now recaptured by British forces. The German crew is taken prisoner (the photo was released later for the press).

Left: The same Matilda again, seen from the right side. This Matilda II bears the British number T 7007.

Above and below: This captured Matilda II tank, which bears the British number T 6970 and the name "Dreadnought" and has been hit on the bow, belongs to Panzer Regiment 8. Panzer Regiment 8 captured seven Matilda II tanks at the Halfaya Pass on May 27, 1941. Three of the vehicles were fit for further use. (1 x TLJ)

The painting of a German cross on the bow of the tank (above) is also of note. That was usually done only to captured tanks, so they would not be mistaken for enemy tanks.

Left: A Matilda II in the Army Weapons Office collection is examined by German soldiers. This vehicle is marked with German crosses. (RP)

Center: The Soviet Union obtained 1084 Matilda II tanks through the Lend-Lease program. The 44th Infantry Division captured a Matilda II on June 10, 1942; after its turret was removed, it was utilized as a fully-tracked towing tractor.

Below: This Matilda II tank captured in the western campaign saw service with the high Seas Instructional Command. This picture shows the no. 111 tank on an engineer landing ferry during preparations for Operation "Sealion." (RK)

Above and below: At the end of 1942, the Matilda was rearmed by the High Seas Instructional Command at Terneuzen by mounting a 5 cm KwK L/42 gun in a socket mount. The gun crew was protected from the front by a shield that extended over the full width of the body. The vehicle was open to the rear. To the left and right of the gun, MG 08/15 machine guns were mounted at the top of the shield for anti-aircraft fire and close-combat defense. (WSP, BA)

Above: This vehicle, nicknamed "Oswald", is seen from the rear. The right-side 08/15 machine gun and its belt drum are easy to see. A group of escort infantrymen has climbed onto the "self-propelled gun car." (BA)

Below: The rebuilt Matilda II was also used by the High Seas Instructional Command for loading drills. The photo shows "Oswald" in a landing craft on the channel coast. The 5 cm KwK gun with which the tank was rearmed became available thanks to the rearming and reequipping of the Panzer III tank as of the end of 1942, and was then installed in socket mounts in great numbers for coastal defense along the Atlantic Wall. (BA)

MARK III 749 (e) INFANTRY TANK
"Valentine"

The Vickers firm was to participate in production of the "Matilda II" tank as of 1938, in order to attain higher production figures or prepare a design for a vehicle of its own. Vickers presented its own design to the War Ministry on February 14, St. Valentine's Day, 1938. This explains how the vehicle got its name.

For this vehicle, Vickers used various components of the cruiser tank produced by the same firm, and thus was able to save production time and costs.

These 17-ton vehicles attained a top speed of 24 kph. The armor, measuring 65 mm, was not quite as thick as that of the "Matilda II." The crew numbered three men through the Mark II version and four men beginning with the Mark III model, as the turret crew was increased by one man. The standard armament consisted of a two-pound (4

The British used most of their "Valentine" Mark III tanks in Africa, where some of them were captured and put to use by the Germans.

The majority of the captured "Valentine" tanks saw service with the captured tank company of the Panzer-Armee Afrika. This company was equipped with, among others, twelve "Valentine" tanks.

The captured tank platoon of Panzerjäger Unit 605 also had up to five Mark III infantry tanks.

The tanks used by the two units cited above may have been the "Valentine Mark II", with 4 cm tank gun and three-man crew.

One "Valentine Mark V" tank with a 4 cm gun was captured and used by the 10th Panzer Division. cm) tank gun, but in some of the eleven existing versions 6-pound and 7.5 cm guns were installed. In all, 8275 "Valentine" tanks were produced, 2394 of them being sent to Russia.

A close-up of this Valentine V used by the 10th Panzer Division clearly shows the tactical emblem of the division (YIII) and the buffalo of Panzer Regiment 7. (RAC)

Left: A Mark III "Valentine" infantry tank captured in North Africa is ready to be shipped to Germany and has had the complete address painted on it. In the Army Weapons Office's collection of display and test vehicles, this tank bore the number WH-056654. (BA)

Right: This captured Valentine infantry tank is being used as an armored observation post. Captured tanks that were no longer driveable but had usable weapons were often integrated into fixed gun positions or dug in for coastal defense. (BA)

Left: A Valentine V captured by the 10th Panzer Division in Tunisia. This tank had a three-man crew, but only a 40 mm tank gun in its turret. (RAC)

MARK IV (e) INFANTRY TANK
"Churchill"

The developmental work on a replacement for the "Matilda II" had already begun in 1939. A vehicle was required with a low silhouette, strong armor and great ditch-spanning capability.

On the basis of these requirements, the firm of Vauxhall developed the "Churchill" type, the first production model of which came off the assembly line in June 1941. In all, 5460 "Churchill" tanks of various versions were built. The "Churchill" was the last British tank developed especially for infantry support. The Infantry Tank Mk VI "Churchill" had a five-man crew. The 40-ton vehicle had 102 mm armor plate and attained a speed of 25 kph. The weaponry changed from one version to another.

The "Churchill I" still had a two-pound tank gun in its turret, along with a coaxial BESA machine gun, which had already been used in the "Matilda II." Beside the driver in the bow, though, there was a 7.6 cm howitzer installed as a second gun for infantry support.

In the "Churchill II" the bow howitzer was replaced by a BESA machine gun.

The "Churchill III" had the 6-pound tank gun, finally available in March of 1942, mounted in its turret.

The Churchill Mk. I, II and III saw their first action at the landing in Dieppe on August 19, 1942. Of the 28 "Churchill" tanks used there, 23 were captured and salvaged by the Germans. Of them, according to German data, six were "Churchill I", seven "Churchill II" and ten "Churchill III." The majority of these tanks were so shot-up that they could not be put back into service. One example of each type, though, could be delivered to the Army Weapons Office.

Additional specimens of the "Churchill III" with the 6-pound (5.7 cm) tank gun were repaired and turned over to Captured Tank Company 81. This captured tank company became Panzer Regiment 100 at the end of 1942, and two "Churchill III" tanks were used by it until the end of 1943. From there they were sent to Captured Tank Unit 205. But since insufficient spare parts and ammunition were available, this unit's "Churchill" tanks were used as targets for firing drills and destroyed.

Further variations had 7.5 cm tank guns, two 7.6 cm howitzers for infantry support, or a 9.5 cm howitzer and other machine gun combinations.

A Churchill III with original paint, but with a German crew. This vehicle, T 68880, was commanded by Corporal Jordan at the Dieppe landing and nicknamed "Blondie." (BA)

Above: This Mark IV "Churchill" infantry tank is one of the vehicles that were captured at Dieppe and turned over to the Army Weapons Office. The tank's turret is still armed with a two-pound tank gun. Beside the driver at the front, a 7.6 cm howitzer has been installed, so that the tank can also fire explosive shells. The two-pound gun could fire only antitank shells. (BA)

Below: As the lettering on its side shows, this Churchill II was also reserved for the O.K.H. Its motor and drive train are in working order. This tank, numbered T 68875, bore the nickname of "Käfer" (Beetle) at the Dieppe landing and was commanded by Lieutenant G. S. Drysdale. The 7.6 cm howitzer was replaced by a BESA machine gun in the Churchill II tank. (BA)

Above: The Churchill III had a new turret with the new six-pound field gun. This tank, seen at the Army Weapons Office facility, is even equipped with an anti-aircraft machine gun. The vehicle bears the Wehrmacht registration number WH-060489. (BA)

Below: With its tracks running around the entry hatch, the Churchill tank is reminiscent of the rhomboid-pattern tanks of World War I. (BA)

Left: The Churchill III tanks that were ready for action were quickly given a coat of gray paint and German crosses. Here a tank is being examined by German tank corpsmen. (BA)

Right: After seeing action with the troops for a short time, the freshly painted Churchill tanks soon looked used. Here is a Churchill III of Panzer Regiment 100 at the Yvetot railroad yards in 1943. (FJS)

Left: Unloading the forty-ton tank attracts lively interest from the civilian population. The Churchill was, incidentally, almost twice as heavy as the German Panzer IV. (FJS)

MK I 741 (e) CRUISER TANK

At the beginning of 1936, Sir John Carden completed the first prototype, designated A 9, of a new series that was intended to replace the Vickers Mark II medium tank of 1926. This series, in production as of 1937, was designated Cruiser Tank Mark I (A9).

This 13-yon tank, with 14 mm armor, attained a speed of 40 kph. The primary armament in its rotating turret was a two-pound tank gun, with a coaxial 7.7 mm Vickers machine gun also at hand. Two additional 7.7 mm machine guns were mounted in two small turning turrets to the left and right of the driver. 125 A9 tanks were built, some as fire-support tanks for the infantry; they had a 9.4 cm howitzer in their turret and were designated Mark I CS.

Six Mark I and eighteen Mark I CS tanks were lost in the French campaign, while other vehicles of these types were utilized in Africa. The only two A9 tanks that are known to have been acquired by the Wehrmacht were specimens used by the Army Weapons Office.

Left: A Mark I CS Cruiser with a 9.4 cm howitzer in its turret and a coaxial machine gun. Two additional small machine-gun turrets are located to the left and right of the driver. On the left machine-gun turret is a warning in French: "Danger, shells; do not touch." The tank belonged to the command group of the A Company of the 3rd Royal Tank Regiment and is seen here at the Army Weapons Office.

Right: Likewise a Cruiser Mark I CS in the hands of the Army Weapons Office, photographed in the summer of 1941. This vehicle, numbered T 7253, belonged to a B company, as the rectangle on the turret indicates. (KJ)

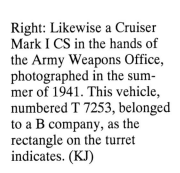

MK 11 742 (e) CRUISER TANK

An infantry version, called A10, had been developed along with the A9 cavalry version. With 30 mm armor, the vehicle was twice as strongly armored as the A9 type. The two small machine-gun turrets were dispensed with. This vehicle had a five-man crew and a fighting weight of fourteen tons. Because its 30 mm armor was too weak for use as an infantry tank, the A10 was utilized as Cruiser Tank Mark II (A10). Only 35 specimens of it were built, of which 31 were lost in France.

One example was at the Kummersdorf test center in 1941. The photo of an A10 with a neatly painted German cross indicates that this type was also put to use elsewhere.

Above: A Cruiser Mark II in the Army Weapons Office's collection, summer 1941. The two machine-gun turrets have been removed, and the armor has been strengthened. The vehicle formerly belonged to the HQ of the 2nd Panzer Brigade. (KJ)

Left: This Cruiser Mark II 742 (e) tank is neatly painted with German crosses. (JD)

Right: Many captured British tanks were kept at troop training centers. This Cruiser Mark II is being fired on with a flamethrower at the French training facility at Mailly le Camp in 1941. (BA)

MK III 743 (e) CRUISER TANK

Beginning with the Mark III version, a new chassis was used. The American Christie suspension that was now used gave the fourteen-ton vehicle a speed of almost 50 kph. This version was designated A13.

The vehicle still carried 14 mm armor plate, a four-man crew, and a two-pound tank gun plus a coaxial machine gun. A commander's cupola had been attached to the turret. Thirty-eight of these vehicles were lost in France.

A captured Cruiser Mark III 743 (e) tank in the Army Weapons Office collection. The Mark III version still had the same turret as the Mark II, but with an added commander's cupola. A completely new chassis with four large road wheels was installed. As the square painted on the turret indicates, this tank formerly belonged to a B company.

MK IV 744 (e) CRUISER TANK

For this model, likewise designated A13, the same chassis was used, while the armor plate had been increased to 38 mm. There was also a "new turret" in use; it had more sharply angled sides achieved by added plates of armor. This tank reached a speed of 48 kph. The four-man crew had a two-pound tank gun and a 7.7 mm Vickers machine gun as weapons. In the Mark IVA version, the Vickers machine gun was replaced by a 7.92 mm BESA machine gun. There was also a CS version for infantry support. Fifty-seven Mark IV and eight Mark IVA tanks were lost in France. More than 300 A13 tanks were built in all. In addition to France, they saw service in Africa.

Of the A13, which made up the majority of the British battle tanks in France, with about 100 Mark III and Mark IV tanks, six examples were possessed by the Army Weapons Office in 1941 alone, though only one was driveable.

Additional A13 tanks were in service with the Captured Tank Company (e) at the beginning of 1940, and later with Panzer Unit (Flame) 100, which still reported nine Pz.Kpfwg. A13 (3) tanks in their possession on June 22, 1941. A month later, these tanks were no longer available.

Left: The Cruiser Mark IV "Manifesto" was also photographed in the collection of the Army Weapons Office. The vehicle bears the number T 9127. (KJ)

Right: As can be seen in this front view, the tank is marked with a white number 4 on a red field and a white rhinoceros. It was formerly used by the "Queen's Bay" unit of the First British Tank Division. (KJ)

Left: Obsolete tanks were often utilized as fixed turret positions. Here a Cruiser Mark IV has been dug in at the Libyan-Egyptian border. The tank has an Italian crew. In this photo it can be seen clearly that the turret shape of the Mark IV resulted from the attachment of additional armor plates. (BA)

Left: A Cruiser Mark IV at the end of a tank column, probably Panzer Unit (Flame) 100, at the beginning of the Russian campaign. At the stern, all the tanks resemble recovery tanks, being equipped with wooden blocks for pushing. The Mark IV seen here also has a special tow hook attached. (WF)

Right: A Cruiser Mark IV tank of Panzer Unit (Flame) 100. The tanks of this unit were equipped with storage cases on the left and right sides of the turret, and thus can be spotted immediately by their characteristic appearance. (HL)

Left: Another tank of the same unit. Even if the German cross on the turret could not be seen, the storage boxes would show what unit it belonged to. (RE)

MK V 746 (e) CRUISER TANK

The MK V 745 (e) "Covenanter" Cruiser Tank was used only in Britain and only for training purposes on account of numerous technical problems, and thus never fell into German hands. On the basis of reports alone, the Army Weapons Office gave the tank the foreign weapon number 745 (e).

Out of the "Covenanter", a cruiser tank was developed between 1938 and 1940 and designated A15. It was intended for use as a heavy reconnaissance vehicle. As of June 1941, the A15, under the designation "Cruiser Tank Mark VI", went into service with the British troops in Africa. This tank, also known by the name of "Crusader", weighed twenty pounds and attained a speed of 43 kph. Its Liberty-Nuffield aircraft motor had been throttled down from 400 to 340 HP. At its highest engine speed, the tank could move as fast as 64 kph. The first type, "Crusader I", had 40 mm armor and a five-man crew. As with almost all cruiser types, it had a two-pound tank gun in its turret, along with a coaxial 7.92 mm BESA machine gun. At the left front the "Crusader" had a small turning turret with a second 7.92 mm BESA machine gun.

In the "Crusader II", the separate machine-gun turret was eliminated after a time, and the crew was thus reduced to four men. The armor plate was increased to 49 mm.

The "Crusader III" was given a six-pound tank gun as its primary armament, while its armor was increased to 51 mm. The crew now consisted of only three men.

The "Crusader" constituted the majority of the British tanks in Africa, with only a few seeing service in other theaters of war. In all, 5300 Cruiser Mark VI of the Crusader I to III types were built.

The first captured "Crusader" tanks fell into German hands in June of 1941, during Operation "Battleaxe", in most cases because they were abandoned on account of technical failures. Some of these were put back into action by German repair units.

The captured tank company of the Pz.AOK Afrika had a platoon of "Crusaders" in service constantly from February 1942 to the end of the year. Individual tanks of this type have also been documented as seeing service with Panzer Regiment 5 and Panzerjäger Unit 605.

A Crusader I sent to the Army Weapons Office test center from North Africa. The German crosses painted on the turret and the bow suggest that the tank saw action with the Panzer troops in Africa before it was sent to the Weapons Office. The tank bears the British number T 15572. (BA)

Left: A Crusader I with the German troops in North Africa. The tank could not yet be marked with German crosses and is provisionally identified as a German vehicle by a swastika flag. (HS)

Right: The same vehicle, seen from the right side. The two-pound tank gun has the same mount used in the Cruiser Mark IV. (HS)

Left: This Crusader II, with the number T 15789, is loaded onto a low loader by German soldiers. The angular plate at the back of the turret is the cover for the turret hatch. (BA)

Above: A Crusader II with a German crew on the march. The Crusader II has a modified weapon mount on its turret but still uses the two-pound tank gun as its primary armament. Only the first few models of this version were still equipped with the machine-gun turret. (BA)

Below: Another noticeable difference between the Crusader I and II types was the track covers. The road sign reads "Diversion to Acroma Area." (BA)

A 27 "Cromwell" (e) CRUISER TANK

Via the intermediate stages of the "Cavalier" and "Centaur", the "Cromwell" heavy cruiser tank was developed. The first production models of this tank were built in 1943, and the "Cromwell" saw its first service during the invasion of France in June of 1944. The "Cromwell" was the most important British tank to see service during the 1944 invasion.

The "Cromwell", with a weight of 28 tons and a main armor of 76 mm, reached a speed of 64 kph.

Its crew consisted of five men. The first types (there were Mark I to Mark III Cromwells) were equipped with a six-pound tank gun, later types with a 75 mm gun. There was a coaxial BESA machine gun in the turret and another at the left side of the bow.

Only a few "Cromwell" tanks were captured by the Wehrmacht; they saw service individually and only for short times.

Left: The 7th British Tank Division used the Cromwell tank in Normandy. Several were captured by the Germans in an attack by the 1st SS Panzer Corps. Here is a Cromwell with 7.5 cm tank gun and number T 187796. (BA)

Right: This Cromwell, with a 9.4 cm tank howitzer, was captured at the same place and is being taken on a "test drive" by an SS man. (BA)

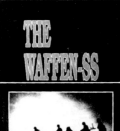